Photographs from the collection of Michael Filey

A Toronto Album   Glimpses of the City That Was

Michael Filey

University of Toronto Press

© 1970 University of Toronto Press
Printed in Canada
ISBN 0-8020-1737-1

Foreword

There have been many publications about Toronto, both in words and pictures, and some authors have overlooked the City's true historical character; Toronto has been portrayed as if it has only been settled since the end of the Second World War. This is because of the dynamic changes that have occurred in that period, which have made Toronto a cosmopolitan city.

In this book, Mr Michael Filey has illustrated some of the benchmarks and the cornerstones of Toronto's way of life and temperament – its royal celebrations, its emphasis on public transportation, public works, and a progressive, sympathetic attitude towards change.

If in another one hundred years a similar book is published on 'Toronto 1970,' it is to be hoped that this trend and attitude will have been maintained.

I would like to commend Mr Filey for his painstaking research in unearthing this interesting store of photographs illustrating many facets of life in Toronto through the years.

William Dennison
Mayor
City of Toronto
July 10, 1970

Preface

To my family and friends

The purpose of this book is to present a selection of photographs that record some aspects of the city's evolution during the period 1860 to 1950. I hope that they will entertain either by stimulating among older readers their own remembrance of a city and a way of life that have all but disappeared or by showing to younger readers some glimpses of the early days of the city. The sense of tradition, of one generation handing its systems and structures on to the next, is weak in these days of change and inter-generational gaps, and it is also hoped that the book will give younger Torontonians – and new Torontonians – some awareness of the city's past achievements. If we are entering an age of cities and of democratic citizenship, a knowledge of the civic past will help give us a good civic life in the future.

The photographs have been chosen for their historical value and general interest, and are generally arranged chronologically, but with some regard to topic. They depict scenes in the public theatre that is city life – mud streets and gas lamps, giant steam engines and rollicking trolley cars, favourite steamers and amusement parks. The captions have been written as accurately as possible and are based, for the most part, on published books and brochures listed, along with the sources of the longer quotations, at the back of the book. I am not a historian, and the work does not claim to be a balanced social history of the city. I hope the captions will add to the reader's understanding of the photographs and stir in him an appreciation

and deeper interest in our city.

Collecting memorabilia can be very pleasant, not only through discovering a cache of old newspaper clippings at a riotous church rummage sale, but through meeting many people who take an interest in one's collection, recalling with obvious enjoyment memories of their youth, taking a ride around the 'Belt Line' or cruising the Bay on the *Bluebell.* I have met others, like myself, who are not old enough to remember a city that hasn't always been a jungle of cars,

trucks, buses and people, and who have been fascinated by these pictures of a past beyond their memory. I have enjoyed and will remember my associations with them.

It would be an impossible task to list all those who have made my research enjoyable and this book a reality. They will excuse me, I hope, if I do mention several people who have been especially helpful in the preparation of this work: Mr Carl Banas, Mr Rik Davidson, Mr Allan Fleming, Mr Scott James, and Mr Ted Wickson. Special thanks are due also to the following organizations and people who have been kind to me during the past months: Toronto Harbour Commission, Toronto Transit Commission, City of Toronto Archives, Canadian National Exhibition and Mr T. E. Swabey, E. L. Ruddy Company Limited, Panda-Croydon Associates and Mr Hugh Robertson, the Marine Museum and Mr Alan Howard.

This book would be incomplete without special mention of one person who has to put up constantly with an avid and sometimes very trying collector, my wife.

M. F.

**1 Looking west along King Street
from Yonge, c1860**

This record of life in the city of Toronto begins around 1860 because it was about that time that photographs were first taken in the city. The first photograph ever taken in the city – of a tavern at Yonge and St Clair – may have been made by a George Thompson in 1853 on his way to Niagara. It is not always easy to give an exact date for some of these early photographs. The date of the first three in this book, probably taken on the same day, can be deduced from the absence of streetcar tracks (laid down along King and up Yonge by September 1861) and the address given for Mr Staunton's store in contemporary city directories.

The year 1860 can, however, be interpreted as a date of some significance in the evolution of the city. By then the forces were stirring in men's minds, down on the waterfront and elsewhere, that were to destroy much of the early classical form of the city which we see in these photographs and leave us today with little to recognize in them except the names of the streets. If scenes like these remind people of Georgian Dublin, a later Toronto could remind people of Belfast. And this should not be surprising, since in 1850 there were more Irishmen in the city than English, or Scots, or native Canadians, and the tendency for the mayor to be an Orangeman held for about a century.

2   Looking north up Yonge Street
from King, c1860

Toronto had been founded in 1793 at the head of Toronto bay near the mouth of the Don. To the east of the mouth of the Don lay an area of marsh, to the west a shallow shoaled harbour, practically enclosed by a long sandbar. This harbour had been the reason for the original settlement and is still the prime natural resource of the city.

Roman legions would probably have recognized that first little town for what it was – a *colonia,* an outpost of military empire laid out in straight lines. Bounded by Berkeley and George, its main east-west axis was King Street. Its natural direction for expansion was west along King Street, and plans were made for its growth in that direction. A fire in the St Lawrence market area in 1849 and the prosperous times around 1850 produced a street lined with a variety of wholesale and retail establishments, mostly built of yellow brick. This commercial expansion affected the lower reaches of Yonge Street in the same way. Yonge was the main route to the north and to much of Toronto's agricultural hinterland, and by 1860 King and Yonge was Toronto's main intersection.

The carriage is parked outside the store of Mr Harry Piper, who later became an alderman, started Toronto's first zoo, and distributed flowers by the cartload among the poor children of his ward.

3 **Looking south down Yonge
to the bay from King, c1860**

One can see, at the end of the street, the masts of a schooner lying in the bay, but not the train tracks which had been recently laid along the waterfront. The streets here are still unpaved with cobbles, stones, or asphalt, though there seems to be (in photograph 1) a cobbled crosswalk and a pile of stones perhaps intended to make another across King; the sidewalks are planks. Under the street there were some rudimentary sewers and waterpipes. Above, there were a few overhanging signs, but the 'age of wire'

had also recently begun: the poles are probably carrying messages to many parts of North America (and after 1866 to Europe) in Morse code. An electromagnetic telegraph company had been formed in Toronto in 1846. Another technological improvement that the city was trying to introduce was the use of manufactured gas for street lighting. Gas had been available since the early 40s, but it was still expensive. 'In 1861 the City Council decided to discontinue the lighting of about one half the

street lamps and to have the remainder extinguished for eight nights per month during the time of moonlight.'

4 The south side of Front Street, looking west from Yonge, c1880

It was only in the 50s that the commerce of Toronto began to be conducted in the single currency we have now. An exchange, where ownership of all sorts of goods was traded, was erected in 1855, and to facilitate credit and trade further new banks opened their doors – though others had to close theirs. Three that survived and grew were the Bank of Toronto (from 1855), the Bank of Commerce (from 1867), and the Dominion Bank (from 1871). Trust companies, insurance companies, and mortgage and loan companies opened offices to use the capital and credit accumulating in the city, and to help stabilize the ups and downs of business. By 1875 or so Toronto had become a financial as well as a commercial centre, though still a puny rival to Montreal.

Toronto had been an alternate capital (with Quebec) in the province of Canada, but in 1867 it became the full-time capital of the new province of Ontario in the new dominion. The new dominion was also a customs union, and to Ottawa now went all the money garnered by customs and excise duties. These duties provided by far the largest source of government revenue (and continued to do so until the 1930s when income tax, introduced in the First World War, began to produce more), and its receipts were shared with the provinces. An imposing new Customs House at Yonge and Front (on the left of this photograph) was erected in 1876, symbolizing these new fiscal arrangements.

5 Looking west on Front Street from Church, 1885

Not all the city was of a noble Georgian character. The east side of York Street north of King, leading to 'one of the stateliest specimens of classical architecture Canada can boast of, Osgoode Hall,' was a disgrace: 'dingy and rotten wooden shanties, and dens of ... old clothes sellers and recipients of stolen goods. There old Fagin and Moll Flanders have their lair; thither, at forbidden hours, Dick Swiveller and Thomas Idle resort for their surreptitious dram.' Also on York Street was the Crompton Corset factory, the first establishment in Canada 'to manufacture corsets on a large scale' – 8400 corsets a week along with hoop skirts and bustles.

MANUFA

6 Looking east
on Adelaide Street East, c1880

To the federal government had been entrusted in 1867 the running of the postal services, in those days one of its most important functions. An impressive building in the latest romantic style – it looks now as if it could have been an opera house – was erected in 1871 as Toronto's eighth Post Office. It was located on Adelaide Street looking down Toronto Street. Occasional such Italian edifices could fit in well enough with the 'late-flowering Georgian' style, as Eric Arthur calls it, but in the boom years after Confederation there began that process of random destruction and ever larger construction which spelled the end of the order and harmony of scale that once characterized the downtown city. The effluvia of engines, steam and later internal combustion, destroyed the colour.

In the latter half of the nineteenth century, horses provided the main source of power, apart from the steam engines in foundries, ships, and locomotives. Horses even propelled an early ferry, the *Peninsula Packet,* across the harbour to the 'island,' as it was usually called even when it was still a peninsula; horses plodded round a windlass geared to the sidepaddles, and the vessel crossed in about 45 minutes.

Stables were located around the St Lawrence market, and cartloads of hay were a common sight on the streets.

7 **Looking north on West Market Street
to the St Lawrence Hall and King Street, c1875**

The Police Commissioners' by-laws in regard
to horse traffic included the following:

'Any licensed hotel-keeper ... may obtain a
license to run an omnibus ... to steamboats
and railway stations, and *vice versa* ... [but]
no licensed tavern or saloon keeper shall be
entitled to ... a license.'
'No owner ... of any licensed cab shall drive
... about the streets during the day-time ...
any notorious bad characters, or women of
ill-fame.'

'No driver of a cab shall appear on any stand
or place for hire on Sunday.'
'No person licensed under this By-law shall
abuse or ill-treat, or permit to be so, any
horse or horses used by him.'
'All licensed cabs shall drive at the rate of
six miles per hour at the least.'
'No person shall gallop ...'
'Owners and occupants of livery stables
shall not wash ... their ... horses ... in the
streets ... and shall not permit more than
two cartloads of manure to accumulate or

remain ... at any one time between the first
day of May and the first day of November.'

8　A Yonge Street toll house,
　　before 1870

The city limits from 1834 to 1882 were formed, roughly speaking, by the Don River on the east, Bloor Street in the north, and Dufferin Street on the west. Yonge Street north of the city was maintained by a turnpike trust that had six tollgates – a system which lasted until 1894. The most southerly gate had been at Bloor, but it was moved northwards, at first because the farmers it aimed to catch used to dodge round by what is now Collier Street and go down to market by Jarvis Street. It is shown here at Marlborough, just south of where the Canadian Pacific track would be laid; after 1870 it was moved further north again, halfway up the hill. Tolls varied from 10 cents for a loaded cart pulled by two horses to 1 cent for a sheep, a pig, or a goat.

Much of the area between Queen and Bloor streets in 1834 was known as the 'liberties' – land that was not fully part of the city but land that the city, not the county of York, had some control over; it served to ease the expansion of the city for some forty years.

**9   The Queen's Hotel
in the 1860s**

In 1838 there arose in the western outskirts of Toronto on the north side of Front Street a group of four attached townhouses called Ontario Terrace. A few years later, they housed Knox College and then, in the 1850s, became a hotel – first Sword's Hotel, then the Revere House, then the Queen's Hotel in 1862. 'The best hotel west of New York,' 'an isolated island in the commercial sea of Toronto,' this hotel was famed for its plush elegance, its remarkable cuisine, and the cosmopolitan air it enjoyed through the patronage of visitors and tourists from royalty down. There were frequent additions made to it, both at the sides and back as well as the top, where floors were added and a central cupola gave a grandiose touch. It was the first hotel with a hot-air furnace; it was early equipped with elevator and telephone. In the field to the east, a garden was built that boasted a fountain; in the hay field to the west, circuses were held and Harry Piper opened his little zoo. By 1897 its terms for a room were (American plan) '$3.00 to $5.00 according to location.' It was closed in 1927 and torn down to make way for the Royal York.

**10   Yonge Street pier
at the end of the century**

Road communication had always been poor
and, before the railways, Toronto had looked
to the harbour for the arrival and departure
of most passengers and freight. Wharves pro-
jected into the harbour, jammed with offices
and warehouses; the arrival of a passenger
steamer like the *Lakeside* was no doubt the
exciting social affair it still is in places. Right
up to the turn of the century, much freight
was carried around the Lakes by the older
wooden sailing ships or schooners seen in
the next photograph.

**11 At the foot of Brock Street
(Spadina Avenue), 1862**

This photograph shows a scene typical of the Toronto waterfront for many years. A lumber raft is being assembled for towing down to Quebec City; but the logs were, by the 1860s, being hauled by rail from fifty to a hundred miles away; no longer were they floated down the Don and the Humber, for their watersheds had been denuded of this resource. In the 1880s this lumber trade came to an end, but the trade that brought the American merchantmen to this wharf of the Northern Railway Company would con-tinue: they brought coal from Pennsylvania, scoured their holds and returned with Ontario wheat. The 60s were the great years of Ontario's 'wheating,' and the grain elevator at the end of the wharf was replaced with a larger one in 1870, just about when that export too began to decline.

12 The Toronto
icebound in the harbour, 1904

This vessel belonged to the Richelieu and Ontario Navigation Company and carried passengers from Toronto to Rochester, Kingston, Clayton, Alexandria Bay, Brockville, and Prescott, where passengers connected with ships sailing down river to Montreal and Quebec City. The company became part of the Canada Steamship Lines in 1914, at the end of a heyday of financial mergers. The service on the ships was not always appreciated: in 1891, it was asserted that 'until a better lake service is provided, with increased sleeping accommodation and less necessity for a scramble at meals,' the tourist had better go by train, at least to Kingston where the 'really enjoyable' part of the trip began. In the early years of this century, Mothersill's Seasick Remedy was advertised as 'officially adopted by ... all Great Lake ... lines, ... guaranteed not to contain Cocaine, Morphine, Opium, ... [as having] the finest testimonials from ... [the] Chaplain-General of the British Forces, Lord Northcliffe, Salvation Army, etc.'

13 Steamers of the Toronto Ferry Company, 1898

The nearer paddle steamer and her sister ship in profile were the *Primrose* and the *Mayflower,* built at the foot of Bathurst Street in 1890. These vessels could each carry 900 passengers – the largest capacity of the Island ferries of the time – and the company soon had a monopoly on all the Island traffic. Both ships plied the bay until 1938 when, with the grievous mercilessness that seems to attend old age in ships, the sisters became freight scows.

The Island must have been, as long as the wind did not come out of the north, a welcome relief from the smoky gloom and sooty air of the waterfront. The Island also had positive attractions of its own: 'the merry-go-round with its score or more of wooden horses and diminutive elephants, and its wheezy out-of-tune-and-out-of-time organ, ... the 'great and only museum of living curiosities,' ... the fat lady from Central Africa, weighing 510 lbs, without her hairpins, ... a real live Zulu with an Irish accent, ... the switchback railway, the shooting galleries, the swings, the machines for testing your strength, and those for testing your nerves by electricity, ... an excellent band plays, and about once a week a little theatre is open for comic opera, the drama, burlesques, and what not ... terra cotta vases and other pieces of sculpture are dotted here and there ... the Island Park will soon be second to none of the smaller parks around the city ... other cities regret that they have not such a spot.'

**14 Iceboating on the harbour
at the foot of York Street, c1900**

15 The Luella

This tubby little steamship conveyed people
to the Island from 1880 to 1934. In her day
she was considered 'the handsomest boat in
the bay and ... a great favourite with the island residents.'

In the foreground (or forewater) is a scull,
evoking a period in Toronto's sporting history when, instead of a motorbike or a car,
a young man had a boat of some kind and
belonged to one of the rowing clubs. There
were races and regattas, camaraderie and
competition, between the clubs and between
other cities on the Lakes and in the northeast
States. Ned Hanlan was the hero of his day;
once in England he was winning a race so
easily that he pretended to collapse every so
often, only to spring into action again as he
was about to be overtaken.

But this merry fraternity was not beyond
criticism from the city of churches on the
mainland. 'Nowadays a man who owns or
rents a boathouse on the lake front is liable
to have his motives ... questioned ... if such
a thing as a camp bed is to be found ... his
friends usually eye each other quizzically ...
A pitiable story is told about the ruin of a
young lady by one of the boat house liber-
tines. She was in the city during [a] convention and was induced to go for a row by her
seducer, who landed at his own boat house.
She was a bewitching little beauty, and her
betrayer was heard to boast of his dastardly
act after she had left the city.'

16 Spectators at a regatta off the Island, 1888

The water in the harbour was badly polluted long before 1888. The city's sewage ran untreated into the slips between the wharves. The water supply was drawn from it by pipes until 1873, when the city took over the utility and an intake tunnel was built out into the Lake. Deaths from typhoid continued and were still common by 1888; people bought drinking water from carts.

This did not prevent jollification upon the waters, or men and boys, at least, from swimming in it. The Victorian lady may have been inhibited from going into the water more by her sense of modesty – and also perhaps by the non-modesty of the men and boys who often wore nothing. Police regulations eventually required everyone to be clad from neck to knee for swimming in a public place.

**17 A Toronto Lacrosse team
1876**

George Massey started the Toronto La Crosse Club in 1867 and managed to build up quite a following. The club practised in Queen's Park and played matches on cricket grounds before purchasing grounds of its own in Rosedale. Its team was often world champion; its uniform was originally a 'knickerbocker costume with white cap.' In 1867 it was argued that lacrosse should be Canada's national game; 'Just as we declare the rivers, lakes and lands once Indian-owned to be now Canadian, so we claim the Indian field-game to be the national field-game of this Dominion.' 'Lacrosse, if favoured by good management and not made exclusive or seasoned with snobbishness as cricket often is, will find it heartily entered into by all classes of citizens.' Sport was much more a matter of activity by the many observed by the few than what it has become today through its commercialization.

18 Members of the Toronto Police
#4 Division (Dundas and Parliament Streets) 1884

In those days, policemen grew beards, which were supposed not to hide the number on the collar of their uniform. One of their main duties appears to have been to keep a sober enforcing eye on the drinking habits of Torontonians, though the Police Commissioners had to reprimand some of their own men at times for 'intoxication' and 'being found coming out of a brewery while on duty.' The Island had a bad reputation for drunkenness and bootlegging on Sundays, when all proper Torontonians attended church, walked, talked, sang, read, and enjoyed themselves without unnecessary exuberance. Others had not the self-discipline or the attributes of bourgeois respectability to live so much for society and tomorrow, and a drinking spree was no doubt the quickest release from the stresses of wage slavery; in 1880, for instance, stablemen were working seven days a week, twelve hours a day, for $5.00. Manifold temperance organizations arose to combat the 'social evil' of family suffering caused by overdrinking husbands. Some quacks claimed to be able to stop a craving not only for drink but also for drugs (morphine, cocaine, opium).

19   Members of a Toronto Police team

In 1883, the Toronto Police Force Amateur Athletic Association was formed, and they joined in the energetic sporting activities of the city. There were horse races, with the riders standing on the backs of the galloping horses; bicycle races there were too, but cycling came to be enjoyed by people who might have been somewhat deterred by the rowdy enthusiasm common at competitive events. Among them might be the 20,000 delegates to the Third International Epworth League Convention (of Methodists) to whom this advice was offered in 1897:

'One of the most popular "spins" is to take College Street west into High Park ... There is a cinder path for about four miles along the Lake Shore at the western terminus of Queen Street. Bicyclists in High Park should beware of coasting or even riding down the hills. They are tempting, but dangerous, and those who wish to preserve life and limb will do well to walk down.

'Arrangements have been completed to hold Sunrise Prayer Meetings for bicyclists on Friday and Saturday mornings. An early run will be made, starting from Headquarters Building at 5:30 a.m. The prayer meeting will be held at some point a few miles away, probably in High Park on Friday morning, and Reservoir Park on Saturday.

'Those who bring bicycles across the line will have to put up a deposit with the customs officers, which will be refunded on return. Wheels can be hired in Toronto at two hours for 25 cents in the day time and 35 cents in the evenings.'

**20 Boys of Wellesley Street school
on parade, 1884**

Toronto's (and Ontario's) public school system is legendarily attributed to 'the work of one man of good sense and force of character,' Egerton Ryerson. The provincial government sent him on tours of the United States, Britain, Ireland, and Europe, and Ryerson administered the system according to practices drawn from these various countries. The normal and model schools (for training teachers) imitated the Prussian system, and the original school texts were adapted from those used in the national schools in Ireland, where, in a triumph of compromise, books were created that satisfied both Protestant and Catholic. School attendance became compulsory in 1871, and in 1883 there were 15,250 children being taught by 1,993 teachers. Teachers' salaries were controversial, as always: male teachers earned on average $720 – and female teachers $324 – per year. There was overcrowding: 'The teachers have not fair play in their endeavour to teach and discipline their classes.' However, 'the singing lesson ... is of no small hygienic use and does much to promote kindly feelings and the best sort of *esprit de corps.*'

21　The funeral of Egerton Ryerson,
December 1882,
on Yonge Street north of Albert

**22 View from the tower of
St James' Cathedral, looking southeast**

An earlier St James', the primary Anglican church of the city, was burned in the fire of 1849, and the present cathedral had been raised by 1853. The spire is 306 feet high and for a long time was the highest point in the city; the cathedral, unusually, faces south, so that the congregation does not face east, but north – 'the least ecclesiastical of all points of the compass, as it was, in medieval times, reputed to be the residence of Satan himself.'

In Canadian mythology, those of the north were 'strong and free,' however, and the Christmas fare offered in the St Lawrence market across King Street bespoke a northern abundance – and appetite: 'huge beef-carcases, rich with fat, hang side by side ... huge deer, "the fat and greasy citizens" of our forest, are suspended, picturesque with branching antlers ... black bear, in plump condition ere winter has thinned his fair proportions ... big pigs, and sucking pigs ... all manner of birds of the air, the huge wild turkey, sometimes the rare wild swan, the prairie chicken, grouse and partridge.'

The lettering 'T. Hill and Sons' as seen in the photo is still visible in 1970 on the west wall of the building at King and Jarvis.

**23 View from the chimney of the Toronto Railway Company
at Sherbourne and Front streets in 1894, looking northwest**

By 1883 Toronto had almost filled in the 5400-acre site of the 1834 city, and the next seven years saw a doubling of this area. Yorkville first, and then other areas - some built up like the 'flowery suburb' of Parkdale and others not - were annexed. This expansion was accompanied by a great deal of land speculation and resulted in higher taxes. But population continued to increase, and the new areas were soon for the most part the homes and gardens of the middle classes. By 1890, the city limits reached in the west to High Park (an estate offered to the city in 1873 for an annuity of $1200 by J. C. Howard on condition that it would be a 'pleasure-ground' for ever), ran along the foot of the escarpment that was the natural northern boundary to the plain on which the city was built, responded to the northerly pull of Yonge Street, and had crossed the Don to include land along Kingston Road.

The record of population growth in the city is as follows:

1834	9,000	1884	105,000
1844	18,000	1894	168,000
1854	38,000	1904	226,000
1864	45,000	1924	542,000
1874	68,000	1934	640,000

24 Bells for Toronto, 1899

In 1884 the city had expropriated a site at the head of Bay Street on Queen Street for a new courthouse, but in 1887 it decided to combine the courthouse with a new administrative centre for the city. E. J. Lennox from Toronto won the design competition, and in 1899 the City Hall was opened. It had, of course, cost far more than had been budgeted; but one mayor thought that the presence of such a monument symbolized that 'the mental and moral natures' of Torontonians were now 'above the faculties of the beasts.' Others thought that the money would have been better spent on sanitary improvements. Built of red sandstone from near the Forks of Credit, stone which was used in building many of the houses on the university's lots along St George Street, it remains an impressive example of the North American Romanesque style. The three bells for Toronto's 'Big Ben' weigh: hour bell – 11,648 lbs.; half-hour bell – 3,339 lbs.; and quarter-hour bell – 1,904 lbs. They were hung in time to ring in the twentieth century.

25 The new City Hall without its clock

26 **Looking north on Yonge Street
from south of Adelaide, June 1900**

The sour relations between British and Boer settlers in South Africa led to war in the fall of 1899. Much of English-speaking Canada responded to this challenge to the Empire with what later seemed a 'jingoistic outburst' of enthusiasm. Toronto's loyalty to Crown and Empire was indeed a 'passion' at this time. In the simple verse of Alexander Muir:

'The month it was October,
The year was ninety-nine,
When Johnny Canuck first left his house
To join the British line.'

The federal government sent two contingents of some 3000 officers and men to fight the Boers. Toronto militia formed 'C' Company of the first contingent; 'cheery crowds were in the armouries nightly,' and the City Council gave to each officer £25 in cash and a field glass and to each enlisted

man £5 and a silver matchbox; it also insured the lives of all the Toronto men who went off to the war for $1000. The city's farewell to 'C' Company was 'a scene of almost delirious enthusiasm.'

The fortunes of war at first favoured the Boers, but the tide of battle turned with the first engagement in which Canadians were involved – at Paardeberg in February 1900 – and within three months General Roberts had led his troops into the Boer capital of Pretoria. The occupation of Pretoria was assumed to mean that the war had been won, and a false report of its fall caused a premature outburst of jubilation in Toronto.

27 Looking north on University Avenue at College, October 1901

The South African war was not over, however; the Canadian troops returned quickly, but fighting dragged on for two more years as the British tried to suppress the Boer commandoes.

During this unglorious stage of the war, Queen Victoria herself died, and was succeeded by her son as Edward VII, who had made the first Royal Visit to Toronto in 1860 and whose equestrian statue is now the main sight to be seen in Queen's Park. His son and his wife, the Duke and Duchess of Cornwall and York, were sent off at once on an imperial cruise, arriving in Toronto in October 1901. Anxious to excel the city's 1860 welcome, manufacturers raised $10,000 to build this triumphal arch in stucco. 'The Independent Order of Foresters built one no less elaborate at the corner of Bay and Richmond. Electric lights were used with great freedom by all the merchants and the business section of the city was gay with flags and bunting.'

28 The Dufferin Gate
Exhibition Park, 1928

Such flamboyant arches were usually temporary, and were once termed 'civic signs of joy.' One was built for the soldiers when they came home from the South African war, but the Dufferin gate was intended to be more permanent. It was built in 1912 and is shown here specially bedecked for the fiftieth anniversary of the founding of the Industrial Exhibition Association of Toronto. Exhibitions had been held previously: in 1858 there had been erected Toronto's own Crystal Palace – seven years after the larger London one and two years before Montreal's – on land by the lake that had been part of the military reserve. Thus had begun, in imitative splendour, what was to develop into one of Toronto's greatest social institutions, bringing families from the surrounding countryside for an annual harvest-time and pre-school celebration in the capital. Until after the Second World War the price of admission was a quarter; in 1912 the exhibition was first called the Canadian National Exhibition; in 1928 attendance broke 2,000,000 for the first time.

The first commercial electric passenger railway in the world operated in Toronto in 1884, running from Strachan Avenue into the Exhibition, making a good deal of noise and 'shooting sparks.'

**29 Bay Street looking north to
the new City Hall, c1902**

Bay Street was not a canyon of financial offices at this time, as can be seen from the
names of the business offices bedecked with
Union Jacks and bunting.

30 Bay Street after
the fire of 1904

Toronto's most disastrous fire broke out after work on the evening of April 19, 1904, in the E. and S. Currie neckwear factory on the north side of Wellington just off Bay Street. It was attributed to a defect in the electrical wiring, and discovered about 8 o'clock. The evening was windy, and by the morning fourteen acres had been razed, $13 million lost (apart from what was insured), 86 buildings destroyed, and 5000 people were temporarily out of work. Gordon Mackay and Co., Copp Clark, W. G. Gage, War-wick Brothers and Rutter, Brown Brothers were among the companies (many dealing in paper or paper products) whose offices and stock were destroyed. Firemen came from Hamilton, Niagara Falls, Buffalo, Peterborough, Brantford, and London; they came by train, with their equipment on flat cars. But the pressure in the hydrants was very low, and by midnight all the area south of Bay and Melinda, east to Front and Yonge, and west to the Queen's Hotel was a seething furnace. Staff and guests in the Queen's patrolled the roof to extinguish any burning material carried by the wind and put wet blankets against the window frames; and so saved the building. As the *Star* put it, the fire 'ate millions in property,' but no one was killed. Valuable documents held in safes usually survived, but the managers of one company opened their safe too soon, only to see the documents ignite before their eyes.

**31 Looking from the Queen's Hotel
east along Front Street after the fire**

The following account of the fire is as told by a streetcar motorman to his son who recorded it: 'My dad was running a relief [streetcar] on Yonge Street, and was southbound on Yonge when the first fire reels went west on Wellington. Dad went along Front, around Station loop and on reaching Wellington Street he and his conductor looked along that street. What looked like a very ordinary fire was being fought west of Bay Street. There was a lot of smoke, and firemen with lanterns could be seen running around, but it did not look serious. Continuing north on Yonge, more fire rigs were met, rushing south on Yonge. Then as their car was passing Fire Hall No 3 at Yonge and Grosvenor, they heard the "general alarm" ringing from the tower.

'When Dad wyed at Price Street to return south, he could see an angry red glow in the sky, but still could not credit the Wellington fire for such a display. On this trip downtown, he carried a heavy load of sightseers, hurrying down to watch the fire. When they reached Wellington Street, they found that the fire had jumped that street and several buildings on its south side were in flames. Proceeding south a block, then west on Front Street, they were held up momentarily by steam fire engines coupling up to hydrants on Front Street. Firemen were frantically trying to find a hydrant with a good supply of water, and the engines were being moved around repeatedly. Dad went around Station loop and back east on Front as hose was being strung across the street.

'All southbound cars were now carrying capacity loads of citizens heading for the greatest fire in the city's history. Front Street west of Bay was completely blocked off ... When Dad's car arrived southbound at Wellington, the power went off for a few seconds; as he approached Front the power was cut off and remained off for two days.

'Dad and his conductor took turns at watching the fire and looking after their car. The fire was heading in their direction and about midnight firemen appeared on Yonge Street, running their hose lines into the buildings on the west side of Yonge. Dad's conductor went to the nearest saloon for a bucket of beer and the barkeep sent along a bottle of ''something to keep the fire boys warm.'' Every few minutes a fireman or a policeman would board the darkened streetcar to emerge a few moments later wiping his mouth.

'Firemen from Buffalo, NY, arrived and started drawing water from the bay; their fine efforts saved the Customs House at the southwest corner of Yonge and Front. To-wards dawn, Dad and his conductor were forced to leave their car when the fire reached Yonge Street, burning out the building where their car was standing. This was the only point on Yonge touched by the fire. Shortly after eight o'clock in the morning, power was turned on long enough to back the car to safety. The weather was cold, ice had formed on the tracks, and Dad was forced to use his switch iron in order to free the car.'

Firehall No 12, at the northwest corner of Bolton and Allen, built 1884.

Firehall No 10, on the north side of Yorkville Avenue, built 1876.

Firehall No 11, at the southwest corner of Rose and Howard, built in 1884.

Firehall No 7, on Wilton Avenue (Dundas Street) west of Parliament, built 1878.

33 Looking west along Front Street
from the Customs House after the fire

**34 Sunnyside Crossing
in the early 1900s**

At this time, Queen Street West crossed the
lines of the Grand Trunk Railway at grade
and became Lakeshore Road, running south
of the tracks and across the Humber. A hotel on the Humber River can be seen in the
background. The Queen streetcar line stop-
ped before the rail crossing, and passengers
walked over to catch, perhaps, one of the
double-deck cars that ran for a few years to
Mimico.

**35 The junction of King and Queen streets
at the Don river in 1900**

A strangely Siberian scene. The King cars,
at this time, ran as far east as Munro Park,
where the local residents, unwilling to have
a streetcar service, tore up new-laid rails in
1897 and dumped them in the ditch. The
old Don station (recently moved to Todmorden Mills Park) would be to the left, and the
streetcar and train tracks crossed at grade
until a new bridge over the railway and the
river was built before the First World War.

36 A paper mill in the Don valley

No matter how unattractive the city was where it reached the rivers that formed its early topographical boundaries, not far upstream were the natural beauties of the rivers and their banks. The Don had been used to drive mills at various locations for almost a hundred years. The salmon and trout had long since disappeared from its no longer pure waters, and downstream it was a notorious sewer. At present only one paper mill remains of the three that John Taylor and his two brothers built, the first one supposedly to supply paper for the *Globe* in 1845. The upper mill was at the forks of the east and west branches, down to which the Don Mills road ran from Todmorden; the middle mill, enlarged, is still in operation; and the lower mill, on the site of the East York's Todmorden Mills Park, was burned down in 1900. These mills were small enough, however, not to dominate the sylvan valley or, apart from their effect on the water, to upset the ecology. They made paper (from rags and so on – not woodpulp) and other related products, including 'Taylor's Mothproof Carpet Paper' from cedar bark, much of which came from the yards where the city paving blocks were prepared. In summer the supply of bark sometimes ran out and a man was sent out with a scythe to cut down neighbouring thistles as a partial substitute.

37 An idyll on the Humber

In the background is a railway bridge on the 'Humber Loop' of the old Belt Line which ran parallel to the river near Bloor Street.

The charms of the Humber were celebrated in the Toronto Railway Company's tourist booklet for 1894. 'There is no lack of lovely places in and around Toronto, but few to equal the beauties in the neighborhood of Humber Bay. A panorama of glorious views greets the passenger along this route ... passing through one of the brightest stretches of landscape on the face of the earth. Passengers can leave the cars anywhere along the route to gambol on the beach or to meander through the wooded nooks along the line ... the trolley tourist can take a row up the charming river or a sail on the lake, away from the turmoil and danger of the steamers ... A short distance further west is another little river, too small for boating, but just the thing for bathing; it has a fine sandy bottom and is deep enough for a swim without fear of drowning ... There are cars to and fro every twenty minutes, and the fare is five cents, or six tickets for a quarter.'

**38   Looking north on Spadina
from College, c1900**

In 1861, the Toronto Street Railway Company had received a thirty-year franchise to run their horse-drawn vehicles through the city. By the end of their franchise, their inventory included 262 streetcars, 99 omnibuses, 100 sleighs, and 1372 horses, kept in four stables at Front and George, Front and Frederick, King near the Don, and at Yorkville. They had laid some 68 miles of track, before the city bought them out and ran the system itself for a few months.

In 1891 a new company, the Toronto Railway Company, was formed on the initiative of William Mackenzie to acquire the franchise for another thirty years. This company proceeded to electrify the systems it had bought, adding their overhead wires to the existing tangle of lines along the streets. The first electrically powered TRC car ran on Church Street on August 15, 1892; the last horse car trotted down McCaul Street on August 31, 1894. For a time, the TRC was full of enthusiasm for improving the system and promoting its usefulness (see the quotation with photograph 42).

Streetcars did not run on Sundays until May 23, 1897.

**39 Horse trough on the east side
of Spadina at College, 1899**

Spadina Avenue was left to the city by Dr W. W. Baldwin in the 1840s. It was the approach to his country house (on the escarpment near Casa Loma), and was laid out to the munificent width of 160 feet. He no doubt envisaged a noble boulevard, perhaps like the Champs Elysées; along some of its length there were trees lining the sidewalks and two rows of trees down a streetcar boulevard in the centre. The first buildings, erected by the 1880s, were 'sumptuous mansions, chiefly of the new Queen Anne style,' but later buildings were not of great architectural worth. Knox College, built on the circle above College in 1875, trained Presbyterian ministers, was a military hospital during the First World War, and then a penicillin factory. Today, challenged by the mass horsepower of automobiles, it seems very fragile.

40   Looking north on Avenue Road
     from below Davenport Road, 1907

In the far distance can be seen the spire of
Upper Canada College. The CP tracks crossed
at grade until 1912, when road subways were
built from Yonge to Ossington. At Dupont,
there was a 'stub' single-track line laid in 1903
that ran west to between Walmer and Kendal
avenues; one small streetcar rocked along the
track and was known as the 'Cannonball Express' – ironically so, for the motorman came
to know the residents and always waited for
anyone wishing a ride. On the right is Wm.
Davies' store – an enterprise that grew, pro-
fited greatly from supplying Canadian troops
in the First World War, and eventually became
part of Canada Packers. Hanging above is an
electric arc lamp suspended over a pulley so
that it could be lowered down every day to
trim the carbons. People used to crowd
around them when they were first installed
in the 1880s and watch them sputter and
fizzle. The franchise for this service was then
in the hands of the Toronto Electric Light
Company, another enterprise of William Mackenzie, who charged 62 cents per lamp per
night; the company was very profitable.

**41 An open-bench car on Avenue Road
1910**

These single-truck cars were 'convertible';
in the winter, sides and windows could be
attached, and a coal-burning stove installed
to keep the passengers warm. Electric heat-
ing was found to be too costly and somehow
endangered passengers; a newspaper stuck
behind one of the stoves caused a disastrous
fire in the King Street barns in 1916.

In summer, it must have been delightful to
travel in such a breezy way along the tree-
shaded streets, with the conductor swinging
along the sidesteps collecting fares. In the
evening, the streetcars lit one or two col-
oured lights under the route sign as a means
of identification; cars on the Avenue Road
line showed two white lights; one white
light identified a King car, and the Belt Line
was known by its single red light. And in
the evenings of at least one summer, parties
had rented such streetcars for private 'moonlight excursions,' the cars 'being specially
fitted up with cluster and festooned electric
lamps, and they travel in a blaze of incandes-
cent glory wherever they go.'

42 TRC Belt Line car
on Spadina at College, 1919

The TRC's 'Belt Line' (not to be confused
with the steam-engine Belt Line described
later) ran down Spadina, along King, up
Sherbourne (originally Sherborne), and
along the tracks laid in 1889 on Bloor
The company described the route thus:
'A better general idea can be obtained of
Toronto by a ride round the Belt Line than
in any other way. It encircles the major part
of the city, the splendid retail stores of King
Street, the handsome residences of the mer-
chant princes in the suburbs, as well as a
part of the older and less wealth locality,
passing in review on this favorite route. Half
way up Sherbourne Street are the Horticul-
tural Gardens. At Bloor Street the cars turn
westward past scores of the finest private
mansions in Canada. Most of the great edu-
cational institutes, for which Toronto is
justly famous, are on the Belt Line, and it
passes all the leading hotels, and crosses all
the other street car routes. The Belt Line
trip is one of the most popular and interesting of the entire system, and during the
summer evenings the cars on this line are
crowded with ladies and babies out for an
airing, and physicians prescribe this trip
very generally as a most refreshing bed-time
stimulant and diversion.'

Other potential uses of the streetcar are described in the accompanying extract from a
TRC brochure:

The trolley postal car, designed to facilitate the collection and distribution of mail matter is now being
tested in one or two leading cities in the United
States. As soon as its practical utility has been
firmly established, the Toronto Railway Company
will be ready to adopt the idea on the recommen-
dation of the postal authorities.

In time there may be a demand for a local and
suburban express and freight service by trolley cars.
When that time arrives the company will be ready
to operate a special service for that purpose.

A partial test was made of conveying the city's
garbage in trolley carts by night. In time, the company, ever ready to extend its usefulness, may be
asked to supply this service under a permanent
arrangement. Many bright suggestions ... come from
clever people, and all receive careful attention.
Usually they are unique rather than useful.

For instance, one idea recently suggested by a
Toronto undertaker, proposed the operation of a
specially constructed private funeral car. His design
represented a long car, finished in black, trimmed
in silver and hung with black curtains. The forward
quarter section of the car was to be enclosed and
provided for the reception of the casket, and the
remainder of the car, furnished in sumptuous but
sombre upholstering, for the mourners. The sugges-
tion bristled with details but – at present the company is wholly engaged in continually improving
the service for live people.

43 Looking west on Front Street, 1916

In the background is the Queen's Hotel, and to the left is an area burned over by the 1904 fire where construction of the present Union Station had already begun. The clustered electric lights might remind some Torontonians then of the war being waged between, on one hand, the city and the Ontario Hydro-Electric Power Commission and, on the other, Sir William Mackenzie (he had been knighted in 1911) and his Toronto Electric Light Company. The contest began with a concern among many southern Ontario municipalities that the hydro-electric power about to be generated at Niagara might all flow to the United States, and the City Council decided that Toronto should, like other cities, purchase and distribute this new (and much cheaper) energy itself. Niagara power reached the city in 1911, by which time Toronto Hydro had completed a distribution system of its own in competition with that of the TELC. In 1920 the Mackenzie hydro properties, including a plant at Niagara, were bought up by Ontario Hydro and associated municipalities.

**44 Looking North on Avenue Road
from Bloor Street, 1912**

Track had been laid from Bloor Street up
Avenue Road in 1903, reaching St Clair by
1906; the city ordered police to stop the
track gangs from working at one stage because it feared that Mackenzie was going to
connect it up with other lines he owned and
that he would move freight cars through the
city. Judging by the overhead wires, the TRC
must have expected to run its track south
into Queen's Park, but this also was never
allowed. The entrance to the Park was ad-
orned by two ornamental gateposts bearing

lights that had been presented to the city by
the Imperial Order of the Daughters of the
Empire to celebrate the royal visit of 1901;
these have been moved east to the Bloor
Street end of 'Philosophers Walk.' The
Church of the Redeemer can be seen on
the right; the sleigh was delivering groceries
from Churchill's Yonge Street store.

**45 The end of the Avenue Road line
at St Clair Avenue, 1916**

This view shows homeward-bound passengers changing from a TRC Avenue Road car to a St Clair car operated by the Toronto Civic Railway. The TCR lines, in various new suburbs, were built and run by the city. In the misty distance is Timothy Eaton Memorial church. The houses built up round Avenue Road and St Clair and in Rosedale had helped to give Toronto its reputation as a 'city of beautiful homes.' 'No city of equal size in America contains as many substantial and artistic homes and so delightful a series of residential districts as Toronto. The buildings are all constructed from marble, stone, or brick, not a single frame house of any note in the entire City.' The absence of wooden houses was due to fire regulations rather than to such a uniform desire for splendour among the rich, whose numbers had greatly increased in the prosperous years from 1896, when the prairie economy started to grow, when the mines of northern Ontario began to produce, when immigration increased, and money poured into the city. The difference between rich and poor was becoming very noticeable.

46 Looking west on Davenport Road from Bathurst, 1923

The Toronto Railway Company maintained, as the city continued to grow, that its responsibilities did not extend beyond the city limits of 1891. Besides the Toronto Civic Railway, other private companies were formed to run lines in the suburban areas and beyond. One of these was the Toronto Suburban Railway, formed in 1894. It operated several lines spreading out from Toronto Junction near St Clair and Keele streets. One line ran to Weston and later to Woodbridge, and another to Lambton and by 1917 all

the way to Guelph. (The Ontario Electric Railway Historical Association's museum at Rockwood is located on the right of way of this line.) A third line ran along Davenport Road through the communities of Carlton, Davenport, and Bracondale to Bathurst Street. Here in 1923, if they wanted to travel right into the city, passengers had to walk south to pick up the Toronto Transportation Commission cars at Dupont and Bathurst; later that year the TTC took over this TSR line. To the left down behind the

waiting room was the Hillcrest racetrack, later also taken over by the TTC and converted into the Hillcrest 'shops.'

**47 A streetcar heading north up Cemetery Hill
(at Mount Pleasant) on Yonge Street, c1899**

In 1885, construction began of a street railway that ran, a single track with passing sid-
ings, up Yonge Street from near Summerhill.
First to the community of Eglinton then on
to Richmond Hill, it reached Newmarket in
1899, and was pushed on to Lake Simcoe at
Jackson's Point, reaching Sutton in 1907.
There were five trips a day to Newmarket in
1899 at a fare of $1.25 return. The line was
electrified in 1889 and operated by the Metropolitan Electric Railway Company. After
being acquired in 1904 by Mackenzie as part
of his power and railway empire, its name
was changed to the Toronto and York Radial
Railway Company. When his empire collapsed,
the section of the line outside the city was
operated by the Ontario Hydro until 1927
when the city transferred operations to the
Toronto Transportation Commission. Picnic
excursions and Sunday school outings were
made up to the park at Bond Lake until 1930,
when the line was closed north of Richmond
Hill. Radial cars ran from the city limits to
Richmond Hill until 1948.

48   A TSR Weston-bound car off the tracks
behind Swift's plant, 1907

**49 The Toronto and York Radial terminus
near Birch and Yonge, 1912**

The first fifteen or so years of the twentieth century saw the construction of miles of radial and interurban electric railways, both in Canada and the United States. From St Catharines, one could travel on these lines as far south as Kentucky or as far west as Illinois. But the Hamilton system did not connect to the St Catharines system, and neither did the Toronto network link up with the Hamilton, though such connections had been intended. There were some 137 miles of track emanating from Toronto in 1912.

Interurban cars were larger than city streetcars and could travel along, blaring their horns, at 50 miles an hour.

After the First World War, Ontario Hydro proposed a radial system for Toronto that would pull many existing lines together, converging at the waterfront and running up Bay Street in a tunnel to the City Hall. However, the Ontario government would not guarantee the bond issue and the grandiose scheme was doomed.

50 Yonge and Queen streets
1915

The financial and commercial success of the city was further encouraged by the increasing use of telephones and typewriters. The 'office revolution' had begun, and the demand for downtown space forced an alteration in the by-laws governing the height and size of buildings. The coherent outer appearance of the old centre city gave way to a complex inner order of office organization within individual buildings; there was economic efficiency within, but visual chaos without. Streetcars brought people in from ever more distant suburbs to their work in ever higher buildings erected on lots and streets that were not intended for such skyscrapers. Eaton's and Simpson's faced one another, and Yonge Street had become the main retail street of the city. Knox's 'five and ten' store was replaced by the Woolworth store at the same corner.

By this time the centre of Toronto was beginning to look like an American city. Its ambition, as D. C. Masters said in his *The Rise of Toronto,* was now to become 'less and less unlike New York.'

51 Yonge Street
   near Lawrence Avenue, 1910

Five miles to the north of Queen and Yonge
lay farming country, traversed by the Toronto and York Radial line. Now completely
urban, this area is about to be served by the
Toronto Transit Commission's new subway
extension.

**52 At the northwest corner of
Adelaide and Bay, 1910**

The intensification of commercial life
brought about by the phone, the filing cabi-
net, the duplicating machine, truck transport,
more purchasing power, financial mergers,
and so on also occasioned the proliferation
of space advertisements out of doors. The
Toronto Employment Agency was adver-
tising for workers, including farm hands.

53 TRC workcar
with Victory Bond billboard

The outbreak of the First World War did not cause the same patriotic outburst as the South African War had done. 'The great tragedy was met with seriousness and resolution.' The Exhibition buildings and grounds were used as a 'boot camp' to which volunteers and militia came for organization and training, and the American Legion was raised for men who came across the border anxious to fight. Women knitted socks in public, and bridge parties gave way to 'bandage socials.' The city again insured the lives of all its citizens who left to fight. Torontonians gave some $20 million to various war charities as well as contributing above the national average to the federal bond issues in the latter years of the war. On Armistice Day, November 11, 1918, there was an 'impromptu carnival'; a huge bonfire at Queen and Bay, spontaneous processions and bands, a steam whistle installed in the bell tower of the City Hall, ticker tape floating all over Bay Street, singing in the foyers of the hotels, and dancing in the streets.

54   The Ashbridge's Bay line: looking south ...

The streetcar line from Queen Street into the developing factories of the 'Eastern Harbour Terminals' was carried over the Grand Trunk tracks on the east bank of the Don River by this temporary trestle, seen here from Eastern Avenue and in the next photograph from the present Keating Street. An icejam has flooded the Don in the second photograph, though the draining and canalization of its lower reaches, to create industrial land and to purify the water and prevent 'fever and ague,' had been undertaken towards the end of the nineteenth century. These wintry scenes have a bleak harshness to them.

55 ... and looking north, 1917

Among the characteristics that Toronto boasted of in 1917 were: the National Motor Show; the Exhibition Grandstand and the 'Women's Building with 18,500 feet of exhibit space'; the number of people 'engaged in the culture of gardens ... [whose] work is conducted along artistic lines'; the number of birdhouses in the gardens; the Canadian Society for the Protection of Birds; the cultivation of vacant lots, sometimes by returned wounded soldiers; 'ten church organs with four manuals'; the Mendelssohn Choir; 'more musical instruments in the houses of the people than any other city in the world'; the low death rate compared with u.s. cities; a telegram from the King to 'Mr Jos. Seagram, on his winning of the King's Plate for the fifteenth time at the Woodbine Races'; and plans to turn the Don jail into an aquarium.

**56 The new Queen Street bridge
looking east, 1911**

The start of the First World War depressed economic life in Toronto to start with, since so many men joined up. But after a while, when war contracts came in, the city's business life recovered and flourished to such an extent that the TRC cars became even more overcrowded. War industries had first claim on steel, so track deteriorated and, despite court orders, no new cars were built. With doubtless infuriating humour, the Company explained that 'the trucks are in the ground in the form of unmined iron ore; and the electrical equipment will be manufactured with all speed as soon as it is ordered.' Mackenzie's franchise was drawing to a close – and, more important, he was in financial trouble for his attempts to build up the Canadian Northern as a transcontinental had clearly failed by 1916.

**57 A 1904 Winton
on Bay Street**

Motor manufacturing in Toronto dated back
to 1899 when the Canada Cycle and Motor
Company built a number of small motor tri-
cycles and quadricycles for the post office.
Though awkward in design, these single-cyl-
inder, air-cooled machines performed credit-
ably. The following year, electric vehicles
were manufactured by a Yonge street company and in 1905 CCM (later the Russell Motor Car Company) produced a two-cylinder
passenger car known as the Russell Model 'A.'
   The poor public transportation service and

the prosperity of wartime induced what plan-
ners now call a 'modal shift.' More and more
people bought cars; most of the city streets
had now been paved or asphalted. What had
been a rather sporting rarity became more
and more common and the fact that it
quickly put an economic squeeze on the
spread of streetcar lines and the operation
of radial lines was not felt by society as a
whole to be any loss. Indeed, the automo-
bile gave many people a new, exciting, and
comfortable mobility.

**58 The Prince Edward Viaduct
under construction, 1916**

In 1909, a planning report had recommended that a bridge be built across the Don in the Castle Frank area and connected by an avenue running diagonally to downtown. This latter was never built, and Toronto maintained its square grid street pattern. But the bridge to the Danforth was constructed between 1915 and 1918 at a cost of $2 million; Bloor Street was extended from Sherbourne to meet it. The idea of rapid transit was 'in the air' at the time, and Jacob and Davies, consulting engineers from New York, recommended that the city build a subway system and that openings for subway trains be incorporated in the design of the viaduct. They were, but no subway trains passed through them for about fifty years: the first Bloor trains ran in 1966.

**59 Looking down the Don Valley
from the new Prince Edward Viaduct**

The complex of dirt tracks may foreshadow the expressway built through this valley in the 1960s, but there were already a hydro right of way and two railway lines. The immediately obvious one is the track put through by the Canadian Pacific Railway when it was permitted to enter the city in 1889, and on the far right is the track of that curious enterprise, the Belt Line. In 1891 there had appeared a brochure entitled *The Highlands of Toronto*; this work was graced with charming line drawings of a little steam train tootling merrily through the sylvan scenery of the Don and the pastoral countryside of what is now Moore Park and Forest Hill. The promoters of this line happened also, it is said, to own some real estate up in these 'highlands,' and the railway would thus permit Torontonians to live in gracious mansions in a new salubrious environment. A loop with a similar purpose was later built out towards the Humber. The brochure ended by declaring 'The greatest rewards of commerce are won by shrewd conjecture of coming events ... Thinking pays!' Somehow, the next year found the promoters in financial trouble, the line was acquired by the Grand Trunk Railway, who finished it and ran uncomfortable passenger trains for two years.

60 Looking south on University Avenue, 1914

Little needs to be said of this most Parisian of Toronto scenes. The statue of Sir John A. Macdonald, in front of the Legislature Building which was completed in 1892, now gazes down a practically tree-less University Avenue.

61 Looking north on University Avenue from Queen, c1930

The monument commemorates the Canadians who died in the South African War. It was designed by W. S. Allward, a Toronto-trained sculptor who was also responsible for the Soldiers' Memorial at Vimy Ridge. The steel frame of the Canada Life Insurance Company's new office building was rising just to the left behind the hoardings – the first of the University Avenue towers.

Despite the good intentions of the regulations governing the office blocks and hospitals now built along the street, it is hard to believe that they improved the street. The value of a beautiful street, avenue, or square is not easily measurable.

62 Looking north on Yonge at Eglinton, 1917

Eglinton Avenue crossed Yonge as virtually a trail on the south side of the building on the left. This is Coon's Feed Store, later the Eglinton Restaurant; the building was physically moved to the northwest when the Yonge-Eglinton intersection was widened in 1922. The track on the left is the radial line, on which Eglinton was 'Stop 12.'

The expansion of the city's boundaries in the 1880s, excessive though it seemed to some at the time, had provided development room for no more than about twenty years.

During the period 1903 to 1914 the city embarked on a second program of enlargement, taking over about 10,000 acres, including Eglinton, and thereby approximately doubling the size of the city once again. Again protests were entered about the tax burden of servicing areas with only seven people to the acre. The building of houses was somewhat slowed during the First World War, but in the early 20s there was a rapid development of bungalows in the west end of the city and in the Danforth and Birchcliffe areas,

and later of larger houses to the north.

63 The new road to Hamilton
Lakeshore Road, 1916

This unprepossessing vista was one of the minor wonders of its age – one of the longest intercity stretches of concrete in the world and the first poured-concrete slab highway in Ontario. It is the Lakeshore Road somewhere on the Toronto side of Port Credit, for the radial line on the right, belonging to the Toronto and York (Mimico Division) Railway, went no further; a radial from Hamilton reached Oakville, but the two were never joined.

The Toronto Publicity Bureau published *On to Toronto by Motor* in the early 20s and gave some early traffic regulations in the city: 'No horse or vehicle shall be left in such a manner as to obstruct the ordinary traffic of the street ... Overtaking [vehicles] shall give audible warning and pass to the left ... [and, rather confusingly] When any vehicle meets or overtakes a streetcar ... operated in or near the centre of the travelled portion of the highway which is stationary for the purpose of taking on or discharging passengers, the vehicle shall not pass the car or approach nearer than six feet measured back or forward from the rear or front end, as the case may be, of the car on the side of which passengers are getting on or off until such passengers have got on or got safely to the side of the street, as the case may be.'

**64 Bloor and Bathurst streets
looking west, 1922**

In 1921, the TRC's franchise came to an end, and the disgruntled City had no intention of renewing it or offering it to another entrepreneur. Private enterprise had failed, so public enterprise was given its chance. The Toronto Transportation Commission was established and purchased most of the assets of the TRC, after many wrangles, for over $11 million. The TTC set to its task with vigour, as the TRC had done thirty years before. Track gangs were soon seen all over the city rehabilitating the old track and laying new track. On a cement foundation, covered with various tamping materials and cushions, were laid 6" x 8" x 8' ties to which the track was bolted; granite block setts paved the street. The track was 4' 10⅞" wide, with a 'devilstrip' (the width between two pairs of tracks) of 5' 4". Mileage increased from 127 to 222 by the end of 1923 (but only to 285 by the end of 1952). Honest Ed's emporium took over the house seen in the background.

**65 Laying new track at
King, Queen, and Roncesvalles, 1923**

This was the most complicated track intersection in Toronto; old track was removed
and new track bolted into place in nine
hours.

The Toronto Transportation Commissioners were three Toronto citizens who were
required to operate the system on a service-
at-cost basis. The transfer system inaugurated by the TRC was continued, and adult
fares in 1921 were set at: 7 cents for one
ticket, 25 cents for four, and $3.00 for
fifty. The wage rates for motormen and

conductors remained the same for about
twenty years – 60 cents an hour after three
years' service, time and a quarter on Sundays, time and a half for overtime.

66 TTC double-deck bus, 1922   **67 A TTC trolley coach, 1924**

The TTC had to replace about half the cars bought from the TRC and acquire new ones. But it was full of other initiatives: this doubledecker, nicknamed 'Tilly,' had solid tires and was driven by a gasoline-electric motor. It had frequent breakdowns, and passengers found the top too cold; this experiment was considered a failure. The bus route was a short feeder to the streetcars on Dundas; it ran via Humberside and High Park Avenue along Annette to Runnymede.

Another experiment that was tried and not repeated until after the Second World War, this trolley coach ran from Yonge along Merton to Mt Pleasant Road and up to Eglinton. The vehicle was scrapped when the St Clair-Mount Pleasant streetcars started to run in 1925. In 1927 the Gray Coach Line was incorporated as a subsidiary of the TTC to provide an interurban service.

**68 After the storm of March 1931
on Adelaide Street**

Fifteen inches of heavy wet snow fell in this
storm. Many Torontonians will remember
the snow storm of 1944 when 22 inches fell
in twelve hours. Clean-up operations were
much easier than they are now because of
the smaller number of automobiles then in
use, particularly with wartime restrictions
on gasoline and tires.

69   Free bathing car
King at Roncesvalles Avenue, 1929

The TTC continued a practice of its forerunner, which itself harks back to the late nineteenth century when the City provided free passage across the bay for children to swim off the Island. Every day of the school holidays until 1929 free streetcars ran from various parts of the city to Sunnyside (and for a few years to the ferry docks). There were two supervised beaches on the Island, and two in the east end – one at Simcoe Park (Cherry Beach) and one at Kew Gardens (Kew Beach). Athletic grounds were provided by the city in 1930 with 'reasonable liberality': 270 tennis courts, 24 lawn-bowling greens, 77 baseball diamonds, 41 football fields, 10 cricket pitches, 7 lacrosse fields, 2 quoiting grounds; and, for the winter, 65 hockey rinks, 65 skating rinks, 16 winter slides for children, 7 toboggan slides, and 1 curling rink.

70 At Sunnyside Beach, 1931

After the First World War, the Toronto Harbour Commission began the development of the waterfront from the Humber River eastwards. A breakwater was constructed offshore along Sunnyside beach to create a protected passage for small boats between the Humber and the harbour and to provide a venue for canoe races. 'Toronto's citizens love to play and swim and paddle and frolic in the sunshine and fresh air of Canada's healthful climate. They have a keen appreciation of the ideal facilities provided by the city's lakeshore location and the cultivation of natural advantages by municipal enterprise.'

To the Sunnyside breakwater was towed the *Julia B. Merrill,* a lake freighter built in Michigan in 1872. The last sailing ship formerly the 'Queen of the Great Lakes,' she was burnt here as a spectacle to attract crowds to the amusement park.

71 Sunnyside Beach in the 1920s

The 'Bathing Pavilion' was built in 1922 as part of the same development scheme. It was 'equipped with every modern convenience for the comfort and safety of bathers. Close to 8000 bathers may be accommodated at one time. Water slides for adults and children are provided free of charge and, in the morning, there are free swimming instructions for the children.'

These facilities are a far cry from an early Toronto establishment known as the 'Royal Floating Baths' erected at the foot of Frederick Street in 1836; it contained ten warm and ten cold baths, a promenade deck, a drawing room, and a reading room. Newspapers of the day hoped to see it 'respectably patronized.'

The Harbour Commission also in the early 20s built Lakeshore Boulevard along the foreshore, with a wooden boardwalk promenade along two miles of the water's edge.

**72   Looking north from
the 'Old Western Gap,' 1927**

This photograph shows something of the industrial chaos that had developed over the years along Toronto's waterfront. In the foreground are remnants of earlier waterfront development – the lightkeeper's house and the Queen's Wharf lighthouse. In the background on Bathurst Street stand telescopic gas storage tanks of the Consumers' Gas Company.

From Bathurst Street east to the Don, the railways and the industries and services that they spawned were cluttered in smoky pro-

fusion. In 1909, the Toronto Board of Trade asked the city to do something about the harbour, for it was no longer adequate for handling the larger vessels and increased volume of traded merchandise. The land around the harbour was owned by the old harbour commission, the city, the railways, and private individuals, and it was difficult to get agreement on any improvements. The city asked the federal parliament for a new Board of Harbour Commissioners and all land was transferred to it. In 1911 the 'con-

trol and development' of the harbour and waterfront was placed in this new Commission's hands.

73 Toronto Harbour Commission Building

The Commission's own new administration building, made of reinforced concrete, with decorative pillars, was opened in May 1918 on fill that stretched out into the harbour. Moored before it is its own steam yacht, the *Bethalma.* The Commission set out to develop a new dock and industrial area, not only round the harbour proper, but also in that stretch of marsh and water to the east known as Ashbridge's Bay. Two classes of society, it was said, were interested in the area – duck hunters and landgrabbers – and the latter speculators were presumably unable to unite and persuade the city that they could do what was necessary to make these 2000 acres into 'the greatest industrial location in North America.' This ambition was another reason for creating a new Harbour Commission, with wide powers over the way the waterfront was to be used and developed. Its powers extended from the mouth of the Humber to Victoria Park Beach. It created an Airports Division as well and constructed both the Island and Malton airports.

74 The waterfront 1924

75 The waterfront 1934

These two panoramic views show something of the work of the Harbour Commission in filling in the harbour to make new industrial land and dock areas in front of the city. Many old landmarks were lost in the process – the Argonaut Rowing Club at the end of the easternmost pier in the top photograph, for example. The top photograph was taken from the clock tower of the old Union Station, and the view below from the Royal York.

The proliferation of train tracks had begun in 1852 when steamers and schooners docked at the Queen's Wharf with rails and later a locomotive from Portland, Maine, called the 'Lady Elgin.' A small engineering works of the city, located at Yonge and Queen, produced a locomotive of its own the next year – the 'Toronto.' A train left for Aurora on May 16, 1853, on the line of the Ontario Simcoe and Huron Union Railroad (later the Northern, but nicknamed at the time the Oats, Straw, and Hay railway), a company which took possession of the water-front between Brock Street (Spadina Avenue) and Queen's Wharf; its station was at Spadina Avenue. The Great Western Railway ran its first train to Hamilton in December 1855; from 1866 it had a terminal at the foot of Yonge Street and a station at the Queen's Wharf. The Grand Trunk ran a train to Guelph the following July and to Montreal in October of 1856. The Toronto and Nipissing had a station at Berkeley Street, and the Toronto, Grey and Bruce built one west of Brock Street. This surfeit

of stations was righted in time, for the Grand Trunk absorbed most of the other lines and built a palatial station between York and Simcoe Streets in 1872. Later Canadian Pacific trains ran into this station too, which was administered jointly by the two railways through the Toronto Terminal Railway Company.

The invasion of the rail companies, drawn to the waterfront like bears to honey, had not been particularly welcomed by the city. For many years, the idea had been that an esplanade for the pleasure of the residents and visitors was one day to run along the waterfront. The coming of the railways encouraged the city to start building up such a promenade, but the economic and the political power of the companies was such that they simply took over the esplanade, and by 1860 young Toronto's dream of becoming a model colonial town, architecturally and perhaps socially as well, was shattered for ever.

76   Yonge Street crossing, 1912

To reach the Island ferries, Torontonians had to cross this proliferation of railway tracks. Up to sixteen pairs of tracks had to be crossed at some streets. In 1907 protests about this inelegant state of affairs were made (but not for the first time) and the city proposed that the lines west from Bathurst to Sunnyside be depressed, and from Sunnyside west to the city limits be raised and bridged over the roads; and that all lines, including shunting lines, to the east of Bathurst be raised on a viaduct. The federal Board of Railway Commissioners supported the city, and the Grand Trunk remade its way to the west. But the Canadian Pacific appealed to the Supreme Court against the ruling. An agreement was reached in 1913 whereby the Grand Trunk, the Canadian Pacific, and the city would share costs equally. Then came the First World War, and more disagreements with the railways; it was not until 1924 that work could begin.

This viaduct scheme was important for the Harbour Commission's plans and was a great public controversy in its day. At one time, road bridges over the tracks were proposed as an alternative – and one such bridge, at York Street, was built as a temporary structure – but the grades were considered too steep.

77   Bay Street crossing, 1913

78 One of 'Toronto's finest' directs traffic
over the Bay Street crossing in the spring of 1914

79   The old Union Station

The Grand Trunk Railway called its red two-storey station building between York and Simcoe a Union Station even before it absorbed any other lines. In 1872 it built this three-towered building with train shed to its north. At a modest, if not perfunctory, opening, it was said 'This building will take care of your business for many a long year.' By 1891, the building was inadequate, and the south train shed and the attached offices on Front Street were erected by order of the directors in England; these facilities were shared with the Canadian Pacific in 1896. The three-towered building was built of white brick on its north front, but this 'architectural glory' soon faded. Five hundred men left from this station in 1885 to help quell the Northwest Rebellion; the bands played 'Auld Lang Syne' and 'The Girl I Left Behind Me.' For many years, the voice of GTR Constable George Healy, audible above the hiss of steam, the clangour of bells, and the shriek of whistles, boomed out, syllable by syllable, the names – Indian, English, and French – of far-away places across the Dominion.

80 Building the viaduct
1929

This scene shows the scale and confusion of the work undertaken by the city and the railway companies to maintain the city's link to its waterfront and Island. The photograph shows the roof of the present Union Station, begun in 1914 and all but finished in 1919, built on the burned-out south side of Front Street between Bay and York. The acquisition of this property by the railways helped to trigger the city's demand for a viaduct to end the menace and inconvenience of the level crossings, especially at the water-front and on Bloor and St Clair in the west as well. The Union Station stood empty and unused until 1927 when it was opened officially by the Prince of Wales. The old station was torn down immediately afterwards.

At the left of the photograph can be seen the arched roof of the Great Western's railway station built at the foot of Yonge Street in the 1860s; it eventually passed into the hands of the Canadian National Railway and was used as a fruit depot until burned in 1952. The O'Keefe Centre now occupies the site.

**81 Filling in the harbour
at the foot of York Street, 1922**

In the 20s, Toronto began to see itself in very quantitative terms. A *Souvenir of Toronto* of 1926 includes these 'Facts About Toronto': '3,521 industries, 560 miles of streets, 216 branches of American industries, 68 parks, 1,978 acres of park area, 40 equipped playgrounds ... 106,630 people employed in manufacturing. 64 per cent of people own their own homes ... Largest Annual Exhibition in the world ... Letters sent out from Toronto Post-Office approximately 225,000,000 yearly ... Residence lighting rate average less than $1.00 per month for six-roomed house ... Best street lighting system in America and at the lowest cost ... Toronto has more capital invested in manufacturing than all the money in the industries of British Columbia, Nova Scotia and New Brunswick combined.' Such materialistic boasting seems unlikely to have won friends or influenced people, unless, perhaps, American industrialists.

82 Ashbridge's Bay in the 1920s

It looks like a scene from *Huckleberry Finn,* but the ship is one of the Harbour Commission's specially designed dredges. There were three of them, and they could suck and pump up 400 to 1200 cubic yards per hour of harbour muck to be dumped in this willow wilderness – 4 million cubic yards in all over the years. Some 800 acres of new land are now covered with coal dumps, oil tanks, new factories, the R. L. Hearn generating station, and the Ashbridge's Bay sewage plant.

The couple were probably fishing for carp.

Once Ashbridge's Bay was filled in, the displaced ducks began to use the harbour itself as a stop-over point in their spring and fall migrations. Wild celery on the bottom of the inlets supported canvasbacks, redheads, and bluebills; it was reported that the black duck had altered its diurnal feeding habits and it was now feeding around the shores after sunset, to escape the hunters.

83   An early billboard

The ferry *Bluebell* was built in 1906, and its sistership the *Trillium* in 1910, for the Toronto Ferry Company. The *Bluebell* was converted into a garbage scow in 1956 and was employed in an activity no longer performed – carrying the city's garbage out into the middle of Lake Ontario to be dumped. The *Trillium* lies beached at Hanlan's Point, with hopes of turning her into a museum all but abandoned.

The Toronto Ferry Company came under the control of interests owning the Toronto Baseball Club, whose team played ball at the island stadium at Hanlan's Point until 1925. A new stadium was built on reclaimed land at the foot of Bathurst Street, where there was plenty of space for parking cars; this stadium has recently been demolished as well. The Toronto Ferry Company was bought by the city in 1926, and ferry operations turned over to the TTC the next year. (In the early 60s these operations were allocated to the Metropolitan Toronto Parks Department.)

**84   Steamers wharfed east of the
Harbour Commission Building, c1920**

The steamer *Chippewa* with its unusual
'walking-beam' engine is in the foreground.
She was built in Hamilton in 1892 and ran
the Toronto-Lewiston route until laid up
in 1936.
 Was air pollution then an accepted sign of
prosperity?

85 The John Hanlan

This small single-screw steamer with a capacity of 175 passengers, was in island ferry service from 1884 to 1928. When she was burned off Sunnyside the next year, some spectators wept.

86 A German submarine in Toronto Harbour, June 1919

The American government sent this trophy of war, UC97, on a 'goodwill' tour of the Lakes.

87 The new ferry docks, 1929

The signboards reveal that Hanlan's Point was still the main island destination in 1929, but by this time it was no longer quite the Mecca of fun it had once been. Fires had destroyed many of the attractions during the previous thirty years, and not all had been rebuilt. Despite proposals to incorporate the Island into the city's road system, no bridges or tunnels have ever been completed. The old metaphor of the island being the city's 'lung' takes on new significance with the present concern over air pollution from automobiles. The parked cars in the photograph look uniformly black, and the latest 'Small' Peter Witt model of streetcar, in its red and cream livery, must have seemed bright and colourful. The ferry stoking up is the *Primrose*.

88 Roller rink, Hanlan's Point, 1934

89 Merry-go-round, Hanlan's Point, 1928

'The Western part of the Island known as Hanlan's Point contains a fine athletic field and stadium with a seating capacity of 10,000. It also has a fine amusement park, and is known for the excellence of its band concerts during the summer season. The section known as Centre Island has a large picnic park and also has many summer hotels and a large number of fine summer residences.'

90   Sunnyside Amusement Park

'If you haven't seen Sunnyside Beach, you haven't seen Toronto.' So ran the advertisements for almost thirty-five years encouraging young and old to visit 'Canada's premier Amusement Park.'

Sunnyside was developed by the Toronto Harbour Commission in 1922 on land once covered by the waters of Humber Bay. Each summer it became a haven for hundreds of thousands of Torontonians and visitors who would dine in the Pavilion Restaurant, dance to music of Harry Bedlington and his Whis-

pering Orchestra in the Blue Room, or swim in the huge pool, where Mr Johnny Walker, the noted swimming pool instructor, gave swimming instruction.

In 1932, 'The Great Wallendas' from Spain, Vittorio Zacchini, 'the human cannonball,' and 'Maybelle's Elephants' thrilled thousands of visitors who were munching 'potatoes in a vortex cup,' drinking O'Keefe's dry ginger ale and smoking 'smooth as silk' Roxy cigarettes. For years, Easter Parades on the boardwalk and Miss Toronto con-

tests were held at Sunnyside. People flocked to the open air concerts at the Orthophonic bandshell or to the softball diamond at the eastern end of the park to watch the ladies of the Orioles, Lakesides, Kodaks, or Supremes in league play-offs.

When the park was closed permanently in 1956, the Flyer and other amusements were demolished, but a little of Sunnyside lives on. The Derby Racer was dismantled and shipped to Disneyland where she spins just as she did at Sunnyside.

91 At the Canadian National Exhibition 1929

The CNE marathon swims had been inaugurated in 1927. This race was open to competition from all over the world; in 1929 the course was fifteen miles, which the winner covered in 8 hours, 18 minutes, 13.1 seconds, receiving a prize of $25,000. The fame of this event (and its prize money) was increased by the broadcast coverage given it by Toronto's first station, the *Star*'s CFCA. One of their youthful reporters, Foster Hewitt, was already mesmerizing fans with his play-by-play hockey coverage from Mutual Arena. The grandstand show that year was an Empire Pageant entitled 'Britannia Muster,' and Donald James Baldock was judged the 'Grand Champion of the Baby Show.'

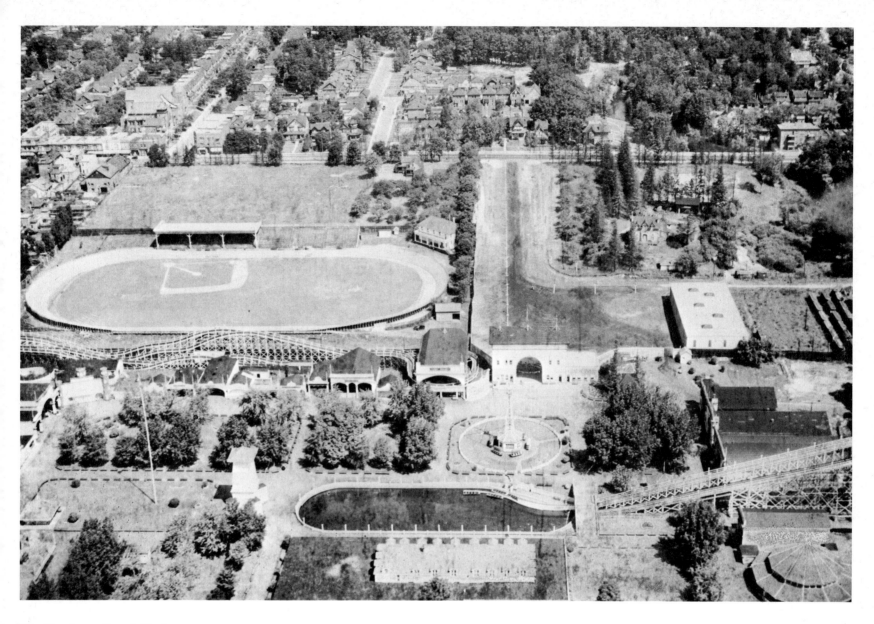

92 Scarboro Beach Park
c1923

Scarboro Beach Park was located south of Queen Street between MacLean and Leuty avenues and was operated for many years by the Toronto Railway Company. Visitors entered the park through a large wooden archway. To their right was a large grandstand and athletic field where baseball and lacrosse were played. Other attractions included a semi-circular midway, a roller coaster, and a ride called the 'chutes' where for a few pennies one could race down an incline in a small wooden 'boat' and get drenched in the pool below.

The park was listed as an asset of the TRC but was not acquired by the TTC in the takeover arrangements of 1921. The park lingered on for a few years but closed permanently in 1926.

93 The Noronic

This photograph shows the *Noronic* during its first visit to Toronto in 1931. Built for Canada Steamship Lines in 1913 she was 362 feet long, with six decks – the largest passenger steamer on the Lakes. In summer she ran cruises from Detroit and Point Edward to Port Arthur and Duluth, and in her off-season from Detroit to the Thousand Islands. She came to a tragic end in Toronto in 1949: when on a cruise from Detroit and Cleveland to Kingston she caught fire at her berth during the night and 119 passengers died. The internal walls were of varnished wood, and the resulting improvement in safety regulations forced other vessels, including the *Kingston,* into retirement.

94　The Cayuga

This famous ship was built in 1906 at the foot of Bathurst Street for the Niagara Navigation Company, which became part of Canada Steamship Lines. She sailed from Toronto to Niagara-on-the-Lake and Queenston until 1957, and was dismantled, 1500 feet away from her birthplace, in 1961. In her latter years she was managed by the Cayuga Steamship Company (Roland Michener, president, and Alan Howard, managing director), but the effective season of two months was too short for the company to break even.

Her evening sail across the lake was one of the romantic high-lights of Toronto's social life, and her retirement left a gap in the amenities of the city.

**95 Moving the Queen's Wharf lighthouse
1929**

For the 65 years following Simcoe's selection of the north shore of Toronto Bay as the site for the new capital of Upper Canada, the western entrance was the only entrance to the harbour. Between 1833 and 1837 funds were appropriated to construct a wharf at the foot of the present Bathurst Street. By 1867, this wharf, known as the Queen's Wharf, extended 864 feet into the Bay.

It soon became obvious that a new western entrance was required further south since vessels drawing over 11 feet of water could not navigate the old entrance. Complaints and petitions were presented to various authorities but it was not until the foundering of the steamer *Resolute* in 1906, attributed to the shallowness of the entrance, that plans for a new entrance were presented.

Construction commenced in 1908 and the new gap, located 1,300 feet south of the old, was opened to navigation in 1911. The old channel was filled in during 1917 by the Harbour Commission, and the Queen's Wharf lighthouse was left 'high and dry.' In 1929 it was moved westerly to its present location in front of Molson's Lakeshore Boulevard plant. Its value to mariners is a thing of the past, but it possesses a historical value, showing the approximate southerly limit of Toronto's harbour development more than a century ago.

**96 Toronto skyline
1928**

All building records in Toronto were shattered in 1928. Erection of skyscrapers such as the Royal York Hotel, the Sterling Bank Tower, and the Star building had brought about a big change in the skyline of Toronto. Apartment buildings constructed during 1928 numbered 117, at a total cost of $7,260,000. The Queen's Park Plaza apartment hotel, at the northwest corner of Bloor and Avenue Road, was built for $1,000,000, the Balmoral apartments at the northeast corner of Avenue Road and Balmoral for $300,000, and the apartments at the southeast corner of St Clair Avenue and Walmer Road for $110,000. The new Northway Building was also completed in 1928 as was the Richmond Street extension of the Robert Simpson Company. The Electrical Building was constructed in the CNE grounds. Although housing starts were off that year the most expensive models constructed were valued at $20,000.

There was little thought that this boom would collapse into the Great Depression after the stock market crash of October 25, 1929. The Royal York did not receive the business anticipated, and there was empty office space in the Bank of Commerce tower after it was completed in 1931.

97 Charles Willard and his 'Golden Flyer'

98 The R100 visits Toronto, 1930

99 Inauguration of Toronto-Buffalo airmail service the foot of Scott Street 1929

'The Golden Flyer' was the name of the flying machine seen here at Scarboro Beach Park in what was the first advertised flying exhibition in North America. Mr Charles F. Willard had shipped the plane in by train from the States; he put it together and took off three times. The first time he crashed on the land; the second time he had to land in the lake as the intended landing strip was crowded with spectators; during the third, the magneto went dead and he crashed into the lake. Like a stuntman, he survived – and so did the flimsy machine. Such a demonstration could hardly have encouraged much confidence in the future of flight.

In 1929 Colonial Airways inaugurated an airmail service between Toronto and Buffalo; a twin-engined amphibian called the 'Neekah' landed in the harbour and ran up a ramp to the Harbour Commission's 'temporary airport' near the foot of Yonge Street. This terminal was closed in 1932.

In 1930 an even more impressive aeronautical visitor came by – the British dirigible R100 after its flight across the Atlantic. It had accommodation for 100 passengers and was powered by six gasoline engines. It crossed to Montreal in 78 hours; its return flight took 58 hours. It was scrapped the next year after its sister ship had crashed in France en route to India.

The first Trans Canada Airlines planes were flying in and out of Malton airport from Winnipeg and Montreal in the spring of 1939.

100 Eaton delivery wagon

101 A Canada Bread wagon

102 On the Danforth

Before the internal combustion engine took complete possession of the city streets, horse vehicles were a common sight, even as late as the 1940s. The horses learned to know their route, and could keep moving along the street while the driver delivered his bread or milk and so on to the houses; they could also bring a dozing driver safely back to his depot.

A centennial pageant, 1934

Episode No. 1
The Governor Simcoe Branch United Empire Loyalists, The Canadian Order of Foresters
When the young Colonies became victorious in their war with Great Britain in 1781, the King's friends in the States were rendered homeless. Determined to live under the flag of Great Britain they begin in 1783 and 1784 their immigration to Canada. The loyal Six Nation Indians precede them, and as the action proceeds the Six Nation Indians are discovered being welcomed by four British officers and directed to their new lands, which thereafter will be their home. The officers then return to welcome the Loyalists who proceed to draw lots for their land.

Episode No. 2
The Canadian Order of Oddfellows, The Shriners Drill Corp, The Patrol, Rameses Temple, A.A. O.H.M.S.
Arrival of Governor Simcoe: Col John Graves Simcoe, the first Governor-General of Upper Canada, crossed the Lake in May, 1793, and began preparations for the construction of the Town of York.

The Episode opens with the arrival on the stage of a detachment of Queen's Rangers. They are followed by Mrs Simcoe and the children and a guard of sailors from the ship. Governor Simcoe arrives with his Council, and greets his family. As Col Simcoe, Mrs Simcoe and the children turn to leave, the Queen's Rangers form again and march off.

Episode No. 3
The United Church Young People's Association
The villagers of the little town of York are pursuing their peaceful ways when suddenly a courier arrives with the stirring news that Admiral Horatio Nelson has met and destroyed the French Mediterranean fleet in Aboukir Bay.

The excitement grows. More people rush from their homes to hear the glad tidings. A small cannon is hauled down the stage and a salute fired. Casks of ale are broached as the populace fittingly celebrates the great event.

Episode No. 4
The Independent Order of Foresters
Brock and the York Militia: As the light increases, General Brock is discovered in the centre of a group of men, telling them of the new danger that has arisen, and that the country is in danger of attack by American troops at any moment. The men respond with a cheer, and prepare to go forth under the able leadership of the hero of Upper Canada. As this group marches back the lights fade, and in the moment of darkness the trained Militia march in their place. General Brock's great efforts have been rewarded, and he and his men go forth to victory.

Episode No. 5
The Anglican Young People's Association
Capture of York: On a pleasant morning in April, 1813, an American fleet makes a sudden appearance, and proceeds to attack the fort. Their objective is the destruction of a ship which is in the process of construction. The regulars, aided gallantly by the Militia, make a brave stand, but being terribly out-numbered by the Americans, are forced to retreat. They burn the ship to prevent it falling into the hands of the enemy, and proceed in orderly retreat through the town. The Americans press on and into the Fort. As they do so, a magazine blows up, killing General Pike and two hundred men. Another group of Americans appear, under the command of General Dearborn, and proceed to burn the town. Bishop Strachan makes violent protest in vain, and the episode ends with the town in flames.

Episode No. 6
The Native Sons of Canada
William Lyon Mackenzie: The Tableau stage slowly lights to a symbolic picture of the election of William Lyon Mackenzie as first Mayor of Toronto. As the light begins to dim, the stage action begins. W. L. Mackenzie is discovered being drawn in his carriage by his enthusiastic admirers, who have dispensed with horses in the high fever of election excitement. The first Mayor greets them with a wave of his hat, but the excitement of the crowd rises to a high pitch and they pull him from the carriage and carry him on their shoulders. He is brought back again, placed in his carriage, and makes a triumphant exit.

Episode No. 7
The County Orange Lodge
The scene changes. Discontent has grown in the northern settlements until the blacksmiths are forging pikes, and Mackenzie is advocating a march on Toronto and the overthrow of the Government by force of arms. The rebels have reached Montgomery's Tavern when the alarm bells start to ring. People rush on the stage in great excitement. Col Fitzgibbon appears and quickly lines up his force of old Home Guardsmen, and prepares to march against the aroused farmers. Just as they are about to move off, a courier arrives on horseback. The militia have the situation in hand, and the rebels are dispersed. The happy populace line up and cheer as the active militia march past.

Episode No. 8
Young Women's Christian Association, Young Men's Christian Association, Eaton Young Men's Club
The Royal Ball: The Ball at Osgoode Hall in honour of His Royal Highness, the Prince of Wales, proved to be a gala event. The scene opens with the old-time waltz already in progress. As the dance finishes, the arrival of His Royal Highness is announced. The Prince proceeds to the raised dais in the centre of the stage. Mr Cameron of the Queen's Bench approaches the Prince and requests the honour of his signature on the scroll of the Lawyer's Society. The Prince kindly acquiesces and signs the scroll. The Duke of Newcastle, his courtly keeper, then introduces the future King to his first dancing partner, and the band strikes up the Minuet. The dance finishes, the clock strikes twelve, and the young Prince proceeds to take his leave as the band plays 'Auld Lang Syne.'

Episode No. 9
The Toronto Fire Department, The Baptist Young People's Association, De La Salle 'Oakland'
Semi-Centennial, 1884: In 1884, when Alderman McMurrich proposed a Semi-Centennial celebration, the idea caught the imagination of the people. Among many of the features of the celebration was the Parade. Beginning with the Civic Council on foot, the Parade consists of a float, 'The Occupation of the British,' followed by the Band. Then the float, 'Landing of Governor Simcoe,' followed by the Toronto Bicycle Club. The Parade of the Firemen concludes the day's celebration.

Episode No. 10
The Gentlemen of the Anglican Young People's Association, The Gentlemen of the United Church Young People's Association
Queen Victoria's Funeral: The death and funeral of a great and noble Queen is symbolized with the simplicity and beauty which marked her life.

Episodes Nos. 11 and 12
The entire Personnel
Armistice Day and the introduction of the great Choir, who sing the songs of the wartime era.

The return to peace and optimism toward the future is reached in the Choir's rendition of Sir Edward Elgar's great work, 'The Epilogue from Caractacus.'

GOD SAVE THE KING

103 Centennial Parade, 1934

In 1934, Toronto celebrated its 100th anniversary as a city. Among the festivities was this parade, passing along Bloor Street near Parliament. An old omnibus, suitably refurbished, of the Toronto Street Railway was an eye catcher. It was painted green, sat six passengers and ran on routes which were not travelled enough to support an investment in street railway track.

March 5 was the last day of Toronto's first century, and a vast watch-night service was held in the Coliseum at the CNE grounds.

Mackenzie King was present, along with other dignitaries, a crowd of 11,000, and a choir of 2,500. The first part of the service was 'devoted to thanksgiving and praise of the Lord for his bounty,' and the president of the university preached on a text from Isaiah: 'Enlarge the place of thy tent and let them stretch forth the curtains of thine habitations; spare not, lengthen thy cords and strengthen thy stakes.' Outside were fireworks, 'bombs,' and a bonfire on the Island organized by the Harbour Commis-

sion. Toronto's 'Big Ben' boomed in the new century. Everyone in the Coliseum stood to listen to the choir sing Stanford's 'Te Deum' and the Hallelujah chorus, and then joined in 'God Save the King.'

A portion of the program for a pageant held that year appears opposite.

104 Mary Gladys Smith at the Grand, 1925

Toronto's first Grand Opera House was erected in 1874 on the south side of Adelaide Street West near Yonge. Its first play was *School for Scandal* performed before the governor-general. The theatre was destroyed by fire in 1879 and the edifice shown in this photo was re-opened in 1880.

The undisputed queen of the silent screen was born in 1893 at 211 University Avenue, an unpretentious start for America's sweetheart, Mary Pickford.

105 Shea's Hippodrome, 1941

Jeremiah Shea's Hippodrome on Terauley (Bay) Street was one of Toronto's largest theatres. It seated 3663 people, showed vaudeville acts, silent and talking movies, and was famous for its mighty pipe organ (now in Casa Loma). The theatre was demolished in 1957 to clear the site for the new City Hall.

In early 1930, Torontonians on a night-out could hear Sir Harry Lauder in person at the Royal Alexandra; see and hear Rudy Vallee, 'radio idol of millions,' in an 'all-talking, singing, dancing comedy-drama "The Vagabond Lover"' at Pantages (now the Imperial), where Radio Pictures' 'famous dancing girls' were also featured; or thrill to Ramon Novarro and Dorothy Jordan, 'the erstwhile Broadway charmer,' in 'Devil May Care,' in which Novarro plays a 'dashing young lieutenant in Bonaparte's army who is condemned to death, ... evades the firing squad by leaping over the wall against which they have placed him for his last stand against fate ... and secretes himself in the bedchamber of the most beautiful young girl in France ...'

106　A Spitfire in front of City Hall

107　Bren-gun carriers on Bay Street

108　A parade on University Avenue

Canada entered the Second World War on September 10, 1939. Toronto provided men, women, and money, suffered some privation through rationing, and again witnessed a wartime development of its industries. By this time, some thought was being given to the amalgamation of Toronto with its surrounding municipalities, many of which had become bankrupt in the depressed 30s and contained an increasing percentage of Toronto's workers and factories; the seeds of metropolitan government had been sown. A housing problem developed too, and the city began to envision more and more apartment buildings rising to replace old family houses. The devastation and slow recovery of both Britain and Europe caused a wave of immigrants to arrive in the city, gradually eroding the British-American character of the place and giving it a new cosmopolitanism – i.e., the character of a world city.

By this time too, as far as this book is concerned, Toronto was more and more recognizably like the central city we have today. We shall end here, confident that for the next thirty years most of its citizens lived in reasonable happiness, leading productive, tolerant, honest, sporting, and enterprising lives as had Torontonians of earlier generations. There will always be problems in the functioning of the ever larger and more complex environment of the city as its citizens and their government try to make it a better place.

109   Tearing up Yonge Street
        for the subway, 1950

References

Text quotations accompanying the following photographs:

3 *75 Years, 1848-1923,* Consumers' Gas Company of Toronto, p. 23

4 C. P. Mulvany, *Toronto: Past and Present,* Toronto, 1884, pp. 44, 291

7 *Cab and Livery By-Laws,* Police Commissioners, 1891 ed.

12 G. Mercer Adam, *Illustrated Toronto,* Montreal 1891, p. 59

13 The *Globe,* July 5, 1888

15 J. Ross Robertson, *Landmarks of Toronto,* Toronto 1895. From the *Empire,* quoted in C. S. Clark, *Of Toronto the Good,* Montreal 1898; Toronto 1970, pp. 93-5

17 Quoted in Henry Roxborough, *One Hundred – Not Out,* Toronto 1966, p. 41

19 Programme of the Third International Epworth League Convention in Toronto, July 1897

20 Mulvany, *Toronto: Past and Present,* pp. 81, 79

22 Mulvany, *Toronto: Past and Present,*

pp. 148, 144-5

26 J. E. Middleton, *The Municipality of Toronto,* Toronto, New York 1923, pp. 354-5

27 Middleton, *The Municipality of Toronto,* p. 362

31 Louis H. Pursley, *Street Railways of Toronto, 1861-1921,* Los Angeles 1958

42 *Toronto as Seen from the Trolley Car,* TRC, 1894

45 *Toronto: A City of Beautiful Homes,* Toronto, n.d.

This book was
designed by
Allan Fleming
and William Rueter
and was printed by
University of
Toronto Press

53 Middleton, *The Municipality of Toronto,*
   pp. 354-5
55 *Toronto Annual,* 1917 ed.
70, 71 *Souvenir of Toronto,* Gray Coach
   Lines 1925
89 *Toronto at a Glance,* Bureau of Municipal Research 1929
90 *Sunnyside Beach Preview, 1932*

Other useful books about the city include:

Eric Arthur, *Toronto: No Mean City,*
   Toronto 1964
Harry Bruce, *The Short Happy Walks of
   Max Macpherson,* Toronto 1968
R. Correli, *The Toronto That Used To Be,*
   Toronto 1964
John F. Due, *The Intercity Electric Railway
   Industry in Canada,* Toronto 1966
J. Clarence Duff, *Pen Sketches of Historic
   Toronto,* Toronto 1967

Edwin C. Guillet, *Pioneer Inns and Taverns,*
   Toronto 1964
D. C. Masters, *The Rise of Toronto,*
   Toronto 1947
J. E. Middleton, *Toronto's Hundred Years,*
   Toronto 1934
Louis H. Pursley, *The TTC Story,* Los
   Angeles 1961
Toronto Year Books (annual)
Bruce West, *Toronto,* Toronto 1967